THE COMPLETE GUIDE TO
SHARKS

Sandy Creek
NEW YORK

An Imprint of Sterling Publishing Co., Inc.
1166 Avenue of the Americas
New York, NY 10036

ISBN: 978-1-4351-6164-1

Manufactured in China
Lot #:
4   6   8   10   9   7   5
03/18

THE COMPLETE GUIDE TO
SHARKS

CAMILLA DE LA BÉDOYÈRE

Sandy Creek
NEW YORK

CONTENTS

BITE-SIZE FACT

The ten groups of sharks are highlighted here in blue. Each shark listed under the blue heading belongs to that group.

Words in **bold** are explained in the Glossary on page 138.

THE SHARK

Sharks are the top **predator** in the ocean's food chain. All sharks are a type of fish, and they are found in oceans all over the world. They have been around since before dinosaurs existed.

The great white shark is an apex predator it has no natural enemies.

A shark has a dorsal fin on its back to stop it from rolling to its side as it swims.

Fins

A shark has a large, triangular fin on its back that sticks up out of the water when it swims near the surface. This is known as the **dorsal fin**. A shark also has two large **pectoral fins**, one on each side of its body, behind its **gill slits**. A shark has other fins, too.

Breathing Underwater

Sharks use their **gills** to breathe in water. When they breathe, water enters their mouth. The water flows between their gills and out through the gill slits on the sides of their head. They absorb oxygen from the water as it passes through. Sharks have very wide jaws and some types, like this great white, have jagged, pointed teeth.

BITE-SIZE FACT

The biggest-ever great white was 23 feet long and weighed about 1,450 lbs!

A blue shark's long pectoral fins help it swim fast.

ALL SHAPES AND SIZES

There are more than 500 different **species**, or types, of shark and they are divided into 30 separate families, or groups—partly based on their size and body shape. Some of these sharks are as small as a person's hand, while others are bigger than a bus. Many have typical fish-shaped bodies, but others have flatter, broader bodies.

Flat-bodied sharks, such as this wobbegong, hunt on the seabed.

Smaller Sharks

Sharks that live on or near the seabed are usually smaller than ones that swim above it. Their bodies are fatter and flatter, so they are better hidden and can ambush the animals that also live there, such as shellfish.

Big Mouths

Basking sharks have big heads and massive mouths for scooping up lots of food in one mouthful. These are the second largest sharks in the world, reaching more than 33 feet long. The biggest shark in the world's ocean is the whale shark, which grows up to 50 feet long.

The enormous basking shark often swims at the water's surface to feed.

BITE-SIZE FACT

The smallest types of shark grow to just seven inches long—but they still have rows of razor sharp teeth.

Female bull sharks grow larger than males.

Tiger sharks can be up to 20 feet long.

WHERE DO SHARKS LIVE?

Sharks live in all the oceans of the world, apart from the coldest waters of the Antarctic. Some sharks spend most of their lives in one area. Others, however, travel long distances in search of food, or to breed. These journeys are called **migrations**. Female blue sharks are known to travel an incredible 4,250 miles in a single migration.

The sixgill shark lives in deep water.

Habitats

Some sharks stay in the same region for their whole lives, and others swim from ocean to ocean. The type of place an animal lives is called its habitat. For many sharks, the habitat is the open ocean, far from land. Others prefer a coastal habitat, with shallow waters that are close to shore.

The bull shark can swim up large rivers, such as the Amazon, and can be found hundreds of miles from the sea.

Sharks are frequently seen in the highlighted areas on this map.

Following the Food

Sharks live wherever they can find food. They are **adapted** to suit the **habitat** where they live. That is why sharks that live in open oceans and hunt **shoals** of small fish are fast swimmers. Sharks that live on the seabed are often slow swimmers.

Many sharks, such as sandbar sharks, live in shallow coastal water, where there is plenty of food.

Blue sharks are found in very deep waters.

CORAL REEFS

Coral reefs look like beautiful underwater gardens. Reefs are very important habitats because they provide a home for the richest variety of life in the world's oceans. But reefs are being put in danger by **global warming** and **pollution**.

Some sharks swim near coral reefs.

Ecosystems

Corals grow in different colors and shapes, from fans to ferns, antlers, bubbles, and brains. Tiny zooxanthellae, a sort of **algae**, grow on the coral. Creatures such as fish and starfish come to feed on the algae and coral. Even larger creatures, from sharks to sea snakes, feed on these smaller animals. The way that many living things exist together in one place is called an ecosystem.

The Great Barrier Reef is made up of more than 900 islands.

Growing Coral

Coral reefs are found in warm water and grow over thousands of years. They are built by tiny animals called coral polyps. These polyps make hard, bony skeletons around themselves for protection. When a polyp dies, another polyp settles on top of the skeleton. Together, millions of polyps form a reef. Zebra sharks wriggle between these crevices to find food such as crabs and snails (see page 88).

Sharks find plenty of food to eat on coral reefs.

BITE-SIZE FACT

At more than 1,600 miles long, the Great Barrier Reef off the coast of Australia is the world's largest reef.

13

SHALLOW WATER HOMES

The coast is where the land meets the sea. This is where waves crash on rocky shores or sandy beaches. From crabs scurrying across the sand to seabirds nesting on the cliffs, shorelines are filled with life. Many coasts are surrounded by stretches of shallow water. It is in the shallow water, rather than out in the deep sea, that most sea creatures live, including bull sharks and blue sharks.

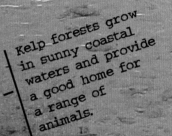

Kelp forests grow in sunny coastal waters and provide a good home for a range of animals.

In the Shallows

The sunlit, shallow waters close to coasts are the perfect places for plants such as seaweed, **mangroves**, and seagrasses to grow. Seaweed called kelp can form great forests underwater. All these plants give food and shelter to animals, from worms and crabs to turtles and bull sharks. Shark **pups** often live in shallow water, as there are lots of places to hide from predators.

On the Shore

Twice a day, the sea flows up the shore and then falls away again. These regular movements of the sea are called tides. Animals that live on the shoreline must cope with being at one moment exposed to the air and at the next plunged underwater again. To avoid being washed away, some **invertebrates** stick themselves to rocks or burrow into the sand. The shoreline is also the place where marine reptiles, seabirds, and many sharks go to breed or lay their eggs.

Fish in shallow water feed on plants and algae which grow well in warm, sunlit water.

Animals that live on rocky shores have to survive powerful waves.

BITE-SIZE FACT

Many species of shark can swim in shallow water. Tiger sharks and bull sharks can swim in just a few feet of water.

A bull shark swimming in shallow water in the Bahamas.

DEEP OCEAN

People splash and swim on the surface of the ocean, but its waters spread thousands of feet below. In some places they reach nearly seven miles below the surface. In these dark depths are giant underwater mountains and vast, gaping chasms.

The Dark Zone

Warmth and light from the sun can only reach about 1,600 feet beneath the water surface. Below this, the water is cold and inky black. Some of the ocean's strangest animals lurk here. There are no plants, and little food, but some animals have found ways of surviving in this difficult environment. Fish in the dark zone often have big jaws and sharp teeth as they cannot afford to let any **prey** escape. Some deep-sea sharks, such as the cookiecutter shark, make vertical journeys every day—swimming up to the surface at night to feed.

The deep ocean may be dark, but many of the animals that live there make their own light, like this anglerfish.

The Abyss

The deep, dark zones of the ocean form the largest region in the world. So far, scientists have explored only a small area of the deep ocean, and they are discovering strange new animals all the time. Below the dark zone is a zone that scientists call the abyss. It is even colder there, and there is less food. Animals such as fish, crabs, and shrimp often feed on any dead animals and waste that drifts down. Many creatures are blind, as eyesight is of little use in the pitch black.

Scientists explore the deep ocean in special submersibles that take them down to the seabed.

Mystery Sharks

Since scientists have been able to explore the deep oceans (using vehicles known as **submersibles**), they have discovered mysterious animals, including sharks. Goblin sharks, frilled sharks, sixgill sharks, and megamouths are all deep-sea species. Scientists know very little about how deep-sea animals live.

COLD OCEAN

There are five oceans in the world, and two of them—in the polar regions—experience freezing temperatures: the Arctic Ocean in the north, and the Southern Ocean. It is so cold that some parts are always covered by ice. The extreme cold is challenging for animals, but at certain times of the year the cold oceans are full of life—so it is no surprise that some species of sharks are found there.

BITE-SIZE FACT

In the middle of winter, the Arctic Ocean has no sunlight at all. It is night all of the time!

Tiny krill must be **magnified** for us to see them.

Southern Ocean

The Southern Ocean stretches from Antarctica to the southern edges of the Atlantic, Pacific, and Indian Oceans. Closest to Antarctica, the water is covered by thick ice and the air temperature can sink to -22°F. Nevertheless, the Southern Ocean is home to animals such as **krill**, seals, fish, and deep-sea catsharks—and visited by others such as whales, seabirds, and whale sharks.

Cold Currents

A cold **current** from the Southern Ocean flows up along the western coast of South Africa, bringing vast shoals of fish. Predators, such as penguins and sharks, feast on the fish.

The five oceans are connected to make one super ocean, which covers two-thirds of the Earth's surface.

Greenland sharks live in freezing waters.

Seasonal Homes

The oceans are always on the move. Enormous rivers of water (called currents) flow in huge circles around the globe, carrying animals with them. That's why open ocean animals rarely live in just one place. In the spring, thresher sharks move north to the cool waters of the northern Atlantic Ocean. Here, they find lots of food, such as mackerel. At the end of the summer, they swim south to the warmer waters of the tropics, where they stay throughout the winter.

GIVING BIRTH

Most types of shark give birth to their young, which are called pups. A mother shark keeps her pups inside her body to protect them from predators while they grow. This time is called a pregnancy and it usually lasts five to seven months. Spiny dogfish sharks, however, are pregnant for up to two years!

A newborn baby lemon shark and its mother.

Hammerhead sharks gather together in shoals at breeding time.

Nurseries

Mother sharks usually give birth in shallow water, such as coasts and bays. These birthing places are called nurseries. There is plenty of food for the pups to eat there, such as small fish, shellfish, and worms. The pups can also hide from predators among the rocks, sea grasses, and algae.

Port Jackson shark pups in nursery.

BITE-SIZE FACT

Some shark pups eat one another while still inside their mother's body, until just one survives!

Growing Pups

Pups grow from eggs, which are inside the mother. While the pups grow, they get food from the egg yolk, or directly from their mother's body. The number of pups varies among species of shark. A sand tiger shark, for example, might have just one or two pups at a time, but blue sharks and whale sharks can give birth to more than 100 pups.

LAYING EGGS

Some sharks do not give birth to their young, but lay eggs outside their body, like other fish. One-third of all shark species lay eggs, which take about ten months to develop.

The dogfish shark's egg case anchors itself to rocks or seaweed to prevent it from floating away.

A shark embyro inside an egg case.

Protective Case

Each egg is protected from predators by a tough case, which is called a mermaid's purse. When the eggs hatch, the pups emerge. Most of them are about 8–12 inches long.

Keeping Safe

Most shark egg cases have long, curly strings that attach to coral or seaweed. This helps the egg to stay hidden among the foliage and to stop it from being carried away by the ocean's currents. Horn shark eggs do not have strings, so the mother twists them tightly into **crevices** using her mouth.

A Lesser spotted dogfish shark hatching from an egg case.

Shark Pups

Baby sharks look like miniature adult sharks. They even have a full set of teeth. As soon as they hatch, they must take care of themselves, and many pups die before they can grow to adulthood.

GROWING UP

Sharks grow slowly and take many years to become full-sized adults. Then, they continue to grow throughout their lives.

Swimming Off

As soon as shark pups are born, they swim away from their mother. It is important that they leave the parent quickly because some female sharks eat their own pups.

Sharks gradually grow larger as they get older.

Shark Hunters

Shark pups are preyed upon by other big fish, including sharks. Even some adult sharks are caught and eaten by other, larger sharks. However, most sharks are apex predators. This means they have no natural enemies —except people.

A silky shark pup.

How Long Do Sharks Live?

Nobody is sure how long sharks live. Most of them probably live for fewer than 25 years, but a few types of shark have been known to live for much longer. Some of the larger species of female shark are not ready to breed until the female is between six and 18 years old. Most females produce young every two years.

This great white shark has a lot of scars and may be very old.

SKELETONS AND SCALES

Most fish are bony fish. They have bony skeletons that give their bodies shape, power, and strength. Sharks however, don't have hard bones. Instead, their skeletons are made from a bone-like material called **cartilage**, which is also strong, but it is lighter and less-rigid than bone. In older sharks, the cartilage may have hardened and become more stiff and bone-like.

Colors and Patterns

Many sharks are dull colors, such as brown, gray, or black. These colors help them stay hidden in the deep, dark water. However, some sharks have interesting patterns. Colors and patterns can also help a shark stay hidden from view. This is called camouflage. A wobbegong shark's flat body, pattern of blotches, and frilled skin make it hard to spot on the seabed. Fish and **squid** that swim above mistake the shark for coral, rocks, or seaweed.

This swell shark has a spotted pattern to help it hide against the seabed.

Tough Skin

Shark skin is covered with scales that are coated with enamel—the same tough material that makes our teeth hard. These scales are called denticles. **Denticles** help water to move smoothly over a shark, so it can swim fast.

Scales from the skin of a spiny dogfish shark.

BITE-SIZE FACT

The rough surface of a shark's skin can tear the skin from a swimmer's leg.

Many sharks have a white belly. This helps them become invisible when seen from below against the light sky.

27

SWIMMING

Many types of shark must keep swimming, or they sink to the seabed. They also need to keep moving so that water pours through their gills and brings them the oxygen they need to breathe.

Different Strokes

Some species, such as the great white shark, push themselves through the water using the force of their powerful tail. Other sharks, for example the whale shark, thrust their bodies from side to side to propel themselves through the water. Their large fins help them balance. They swim much more slowly as they don't need to chase after their prey.

Some shark species prefer to swim in groups while hunting.

Shaped for Speed

The fastest sharks, such as the mackerel sharks, usually have a teardrop-shaped body and a crescent-shaped tail. This is similar to a fast-swimming tuna fish. Slower sharks, such as frilled sharks, are longer and more slender, and have longer tail fins.

At night, Port Jackson sharks stop swimming and sink to the seabed.

Large pectoral fins behind the gill slits help with balance.

Changing Direction

Sharks cannot swim backward because their large pectoral fins are not able to bend upward like other fish. If a shark needs to move backward, it allows itself to be carried back by the water or it swims back around in a circle.

WHAT DO SHARKS EAT?

Sharks are predators. This means that they hunt and eat other animals, from dolphins to little shrimp-like krill. They are the top predators in the ocean's food chain.

Whale sharks are huge, so they need to eat large amounts of small fish and krill to survive.

Varied Diet

Although sharks eat a variety of foods, their diet is made up of mainly fish and invertebrates, such as squid and octopuses. Larger sharks catch bigger prey, including turtles, seals, and even dolphins. Some sharks eat animals that live on the seabed, such as crabs, starfish, sea urchins, and sea anemones.

This large shark is surrounded by smaller fish. Fish is a favorite food of most sharks.

How Much Do Sharks Eat?

Sharks are cold-blooded animals, which means they burn energy at a lower rate. This means that sharks do not have to eat as often as people think. Some sharks can have a huge meal and then not eat again for weeks.

BITE-SIZE FACT

Some deep-sea sharks have chemicals in their skin, which they use to make light in order to attract prey.

Feeding Frenzy

When sharks find their prey, they sometimes go into a feeding frenzy. This behavior happens when they find a group of injured or trapped fish, or another large source of food near the shore. The sharks become very excited and thrash around in the water, before moving in for the kill.

Reef sharks in a feeding frenzy.

SHARK TEETH

A shark's teeth can be big or small, sharp or blunt, jagged or smooth. The shape of a shark's teeth depends on the type of food it eats, and the shark's age. Flat teeth are suitable for crunching snails, crabs, and sea urchins, while jagged teeth are ideal for chewing larger animals. A shark's jaws are only loosely connected to its skull, so it can open its mouth extremely wide to swallow large prey.

BITE-SIZE FACT

The great white shark has about 300 teeth in its huge mouth.

Changing Teeth

Young sharks may have spear-like teeth for piercing small fish. But, as they get older, their teeth grow flatter, and better at taking chunks out of big prey.

The tooth of a great white shark.

Types of Teeth

Horn sharks have broad teeth that are good for crunching shells. But sandtiger sharks have dagger-like teeth for stabbing slippery fish and squid. Teeth with jagged edges—like those of a great white shark—are good for cutting.

An adult sand tiger shark.

Replacing Teeth

Shark pups are born with a full set of teeth already in place. They are the same as adult teeth, but smaller. All sharks have several rows of teeth, but they mainly use just the front row when feeding. The other rows are replacement teeth, to use when the original teeth wear away or fall out. Some types of shark use as many as 30,000 teeth during their lifetime.

HOW DO SHARKS HUNT?

Sharks are among the most awesome—and successful—of all hunters. While some combine strength and speed to overcome their prey, others rely on camouflage, stealth, and ambushes. Whatever their style of hunting, all sharks rely on their superb senses.

Hunting in groups helps sharks catch prey.

BITE-SIZE FACT

After eating a large meal weighing 65 lbs, a great white shark will not need to eat for another 45 days.

Hunting Groups

Although most sharks hunt alone, a few species work together to hunt in groups. A pack of sand tiger sharks, for example, has been seen to herd a **school** of bluefish into shallow water, where the fish became stranded. As the fish floundered, the shark pack raced in to attack. Whitetip reef sharks, silky sharks, bronze whalers, dusky sharks, and some dogfish sharks also hunt in packs.

Stealth and Speed

Fast-swimming hunters often lurk in deep waters, waiting for the right moment to turn up the speed. They swim beneath their prey, hidden in the darkness before suddenly surging upwards. Their unsuspecting prey has no time to escape their mighty jaws.

Thresher sharks hunt a shoal of fish then thrash at them with their whip-like tail. They often work in pairs.

Finding Prey

Sharks use all of their senses, such as sight, smell, and a special electro-sense, to detect prey in the vast ocean. Some sharks focus on particular animals, such as squid, fish, or shellfish—but many are less fussy.

Gray reef shark hunting a large **baitfish ball**

SCAVENGERS

A scavenger is an animal that eats dead animals or plants, or other food that might be considered garbage. Some animals that **scavenge** get most of their food this way, but all sharks that scavenge rely on hunting to get most of their food.

BITE-SIZE FACT

Sharks sometimes steal dead or dying fish from nets and fishing lines.

Tiger sharks mostly hunt living animals, but they are scavengers because their varied diet also includes dead animals.

Free Meal

Hunting, chasing, catching, and killing an animal is dangerous for a predator, and uses a lot of energy. Eating a carcass is much easier, so it is no wonder that sharks may eat a "free" meal if they find one. If a scavenging shark eats something that gives it a stomachache it can turn its stomach inside out and push the troubling thing out of its mouth.

A bull shark
feeding on
a carcass.

Unfussy Eaters

Tiger sharks, Mexican horn sharks,
and Greenland sharks are well-known
scavengers, but great white sharks also
feast on a free meal when they can get
it. Dead whales are a good source of
protein and fat, so although great whites
do not normally hunt whales they will take
bites out of a floating whale **carcass** if
they find one.

Shark eating
dead whale.

PLANKTON EATERS

There are about 500 species of shark, but only three of them are plankton eaters. They feed on tiny ocean animals and plants, which are known as **plankton.** The way they eat is called **filter feeding.**

The whale shark's enormous gill slits stretch almost all the way around its head.

A magnified view of plankton.

Food for Giants

Plankton includes baby fish, shrimp, and little animals called copepods. It also contains baby starfish, squid, and octopuses, which are smaller than a finger. Filter feeding sharks also eat small fish and jellyfish.

Friendly Fish

Whale sharks, megamouth sharks, and basking sharks are filter feeders. They are all large, slow-moving sharks and harmless to humans. Filter feeding sharks dive into deep water in the day, and swim to the surface at night to feed.

Basking shark

BITE-SIZE FACT

About 240,000 gallons of water pass through the enormous gills of the basking shark every hour when it is feeding.

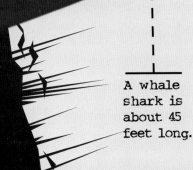

A whale shark is about 45 feet long.

Scoop and Suck

A filter feeding shark feeds by swimming steadily forward with its huge mouth wide open, scooping up water and plankton as it goes. The seawater flows through their gills, where it is filtered. Then the shark eats the food that is trapped in the gills.

SHARK SENSES

Animals use their senses to get information about what is going on around them. Sharks have relatively large brains and seven main senses: sight, hearing, electro-sense, smell, taste, touch, and a pressure sense that allows them to detect movement.

Sharks have a super sensitive sense of smell. They can sniff out one part of blood in one million parts of water.

Some sharks that live on the seafloor have hanging tendrils, called barbels. They use these to touch and taste the seabed like this carpet shark.

Smell and Taste

The senses of smell and taste are extremely important to sharks. They help a shark to find prey, but also to find mates. A shark's **nostrils** are on the underside of its **snout**, in front of its mouth. The taste buds are on the tongue.

Vision

Most sharks have good eyesight and can see near and far. Many species can also see color. Sharks that live in deeper water, like broadnose sevengill sharks, have large eyes to help them detect what little light there is. Most sharks do not have eyelids, but some have a special lower eyelid that protects the eyeball, especially during an attack.

A broadnose sevengill shark in deep water.

BITE-SIZE FACT

Some sharks may be able to track their prey by smell from up to a mile away.

Special Sense

Animals produce electricity in their muscles. Sharks can sense this using tiny, sensitive pores around their snout. They are called **ampullae of Lorenzini**. Sharks use this sense to find prey, even fish that are lying under a layer of sand on the seabed. Hammerhead sharks have a particularly strong electro-sense.

41

SENSING MOVEMENT

Sharks use changes in pressure to get detailed information about their surroundings. These changes in pressure help them hear, and find out if another animal is approaching.

Hearing

Lateral line

Taste

Skin (touch)

Movement

Sharks have a special sense organ called the **lateral line system**. It runs down each side of the body and around the head. It is lined with hairs that detect changes in pressure (vibrations) caused by water currents, and by other animals moving in the water.

Sounds

Sound is heard when vibrations affect the inner ears, which are inside the shark's head (sharks do not have outer ears). They are very sensitive to sound, especially low, deep sounds that can travel far in water. Sharks can figure out what direction sounds are coming from.

BITE-SIZE FACT

Injured animals give off stronger chemical and electrical signals than healthy animals.

Gray nurse shark.

Working Together

Sharks use all of their senses to find out about the world around them. Their brains process all the information they receive from their sense organs to create a "picture" of other animals nearby. The predators can then decide what action to take.

SMART SHARKS

Scientists have discovered that sharks are intelligent fish, and that some sharks—such as the carpet, mackerel, and ground sharks—have brains that are as big and complex as some birds and mammals. Hammerheads are probably the most intelligent of all sharks.

At some tourist sites, sharks have learned that food will be put out for them every day. When they arrive to feed, divers are ready to photograph them.

Curious Fish

Many shark experts agree that great whites are curious sharks because they pop their heads out of water to see what is happening on the experts' boats. Great whites have also been seen to hunt and even play together.

Sharks in aquariums learn when it is feeding time.

Whale shark sucking on a fishing net from a boat

BITE-SIZE FACT

Sharks may nudge and butt divers, because they have learned that divers sometimes give them food.

Learning to Behave

The most intelligent animals can learn from experience, change their behavior, and have good memories. Some sharks learn to follow fishing boats, so they can scavenge any dead fish thrown overboard. They have even been taught to travel through a maze to reach food in an **aquarium**. Some sharks have learned that they will be given food when a certain sound is made—and they can remember this signal many months later.

FRIEND OR FOE?

Remoras, or sharksuckers, grab onto sharks with their sucking mouth to hitch a ride.

Parasites are animals that live on, or in, the body of another animal—the host—usually causing it harm. Many sharks have parasites, such as lice or worms, which can cause them pain or make them sick, although some visitors are more welcome.

BITE-SIZE FACT

Cookiecutter sharks have been known to attack submarines, mistaking them for large fish or whales!

Cookiecutter Shark

The little cookiecutter shark lives in the deep waters of the Atlantic and Pacific Oceans and is the only known parasitic shark. It uses its sucker-like mouth to grab onto another animal before sinking its teeth in. It quickly twists its body to bite off a lump of flesh (see page 78.)

Cleaner Fish

Wrasse are small fish that live in and around coral reefs. They are known as cleaner wrasse, because they like to nibble bits of dead skin or parasites from the bodies of other animals. Some sharks visit the coral reefs where wrasse gather to encourage the wrasse to nibble at their parasites.

Blue streak wrasse fish cleaning a giant **moray.**

A short-tail nurse shark swims with remora fish.

Remoras

Remora fish are also known as sharksuckers. They clean sharks, keeping parasites off their skin and eating leftover food. If there are many remoras on one shark they will slow it down, and the shark will have to work harder to swim.

47

CLOSE COUSINS

Skates, rays, and deep-sea chimaeras belong to the same group of fish as sharks. Like sharks, they have skeletons made of cartilage, not bone. They have teeth that are replaced throughout their lives, and their skin is covered in tooth-like scales.

The common skate is the world's largest skate, growing up to 8 feet long.

Colorful Skates

Skates live in oceans around the world, in shallow water and close to the shore. They have wide, flat bodies and are often highly colored and patterned, so they are well camouflaged on the seabed, where they stay most of the time.

Skates lie in wait for their prey, or bury themselves under sand and **gravel**, so they are completely hidden from view.

Rays

With their large, flat bodies, rays look similar to skates. However, unlike skates, they give birth to live young. Rays are usually larger than skates, and are kite-shaped. They have whip-like tails with one or two stinging spines, which they use to defend themselves if attacked. Electric rays can even use electricity, which their body makes, to attack their prey. A single flash of electricity can stun, or even kill, another fish—and can give a human a nasty shock.

BITE-SIZE FACT

Skates swim by gently rolling their enormous pectoral fins, and gliding gracefully through the water.

A stingray swims along the ocean floor.

Stingrays

A stingray has a venomous spine near the base of its tail. Stingrays live in tropical seas and often rest on the seabed. If disturbed, a stingray will lash out with its tail. The stings are painful to humans, but rarely deadly.

SHARK ATTACK

Many people are scared of being attacked by sharks when they are in the ocean, but most sharks are harmless. Only about 40 species have been known to attack humans. Attacks are most likely at sunrise or sunset because these are the times that sharks usually hunt.

BITE-SIZE FACT

Worldwide, there have been only about 225 unprovoked shark attacks on divers in the last 100 years.

Great white shark attacking a seal.

Beware

The world's three most dangerous sharks are the great white, tiger, and bull shark. In some parts of the world, such as Australia and South Africa, many beaches are protected by shark nets. The nets allow small fish to swim to the shore, but they prevent big predators from getting close to areas where people swim.

Shark nets stop sharks from getting too close to the coast.

Shark Attacks

Occasionally, sharks attack humans because they mistake them for other animals. If an injured person in the water was bleeding, for example, a shark would be attracted to the scent of the blood. Usually, if a shark does attack a person, it nudges or bites them. Then, it will swim away when it realizes it has made a mistake.

A great white shark.

SHARK GROUPS

Scientists sort the many species of shark into ten separate groups. The sharks are sorted into these groups based on their body shape, their lifestyle, and—most importantly—how closely they are related to one another. Sorting animals into different groups is called taxonomy, or classification.

Dogfish sharks are found in almost all parts of the world.

Ten Groups

The ten groups of sharks are: sawsharks, angelsharks, bramble sharks, bullhead sharks, cow sharks, frilled sharks, dogfish sharks, carpet sharks, ground sharks, and mackerel sharks.

Bullhead sharks are rarely more than three feet long.

Close Relatives

Sometimes, sharks in one group may not look alike, or have similar lifestyles, even though they are closely related. For example, the slow-moving, massive basking shark is a mackerel shark, just like the fast and ferocious great white shark!

Basking shark.

Great white shark.

Names

Every species of shark has an ordinary name, such as "bull shark" and a scientific name. The scientific name is used by shark experts to make sure that, whatever their own language, they are talking or writing about the same species. The Latin, or scientific, name for bull shark is "Carcharhinus leucas."

53

SAWSHARKS

Sawsharks have small, flat bodies because they live on the seabed and swim close to the bottom, where they hunt for small fish, squid, and shrimp. A sawshark's long nose is called a saw and is lined with long, sharp teeth. Long feelers on the saw, called barbels, are used for touch. They also have teeth in their jaws, which they use for biting.

Sawsharks have large eyes.

Mystery Sharks

Nine species of sawsharks have been discovered, but these are mysterious fish that are rarely seen, so there may be more species yet to find. They are slender and small, rarely growing more than 28 inches long. They live in just a few coastal regions of the Indian, Pacific, and Atlantic Oceans.

Funny Face

The longnose sawshark is a small shark that has a peculiar snout that makes up more than one quarter of its whole body length. The shark uses its strange nose, called a rostrum, as a lethal weapon and to detect prey.

Electric Sense

A sawshark uses its saw to swipe at its prey, or to rake through mud and dislodge animals hiding there. The saw has another great use too—it can detect electricity. All animals use electricity to make their muscles work, and sharks have a super-sense that helps them to detect it.

The sides of the long nose are lined with rows of teeth.

As they cruise along the seabed, sawsharks use their barbels to detect prey hidden in the sand and mud

ANGELSHARKS

Angelsharks have broad, flat bodies. They look more like rays or skates than sharks, with blunt snouts and wing-like fins. They are often patterned on their dorsal sides, and pale underneath.

Angelsharks are camouflaged on the seabed.

Monkfish

Angelsharks are sometimes also called monkfish. They are strong swimmers but usually live near the seabed and only swim in short spurts. Angelsharks often hunt at night and have tough teeth for grinding up the shells of sea creatures such as crabs and whelks.

Endangered

Most angelsharks live in coastal areas of the Atlantic and Pacific Oceans. They were once common, but now half of all angelshark species are on a list of endangered animals because they are fished for food and their skin is used to make leather. (Leather made from shark, ray, or skate skin is called shagreen.)

Angelsharks have two dorsal fins. Their gill slits are on the underside of their body.

BITE-SIZE FACT

The pectoral fins of an angelshark are very large, and look like wings. That is why they are named after angels.

Angelsharks bury themselves in sand. This one is almost invisible!

Bottom Dwellers

There are about 20 species of angelsharks. They live in the northeast Atlantic and Mediterranean Sea, near the coast. Angelsharks bury their bodies beneath sand and mud and wait for prey to pass.

BRAMBLE AND BULLHEAD SHARKS

Bramble sharks are rare and unusual sharks. It is thought that this species of shark catches its prey by sucking it in, and then expanding its mouth to create a vacuum that pulls it in even further. Bramble sharks and prickly sharks are sometimes placed in the dogfish shark group.

Bullhead sharks can grow to about 6 feet long, but most are much smaller.

Bullhead Sharks

There are nine species of bullhead shark. These small but bulky sharks live around rocky corals and appear to wiggle as they swim near the seabed. Their large heads are packed with strong teeth for crushing shells and bones.

Bramble Sharks

There are just two species in this group: the bramble shark and the prickly shark. A bramble shark can give birth to more than 20 pups, but its cousin, the prickly shark, can have more than 100 pups at a time. They are shy sharks that prefer to swim in deep water where they feed on other sharks, octopuses, and squid.

The crested bullhead shark has distinctive high ridges over its eyes.

BITE-SIZE FACT

A bramble shark's skin is covered in thorn-like denticles, so it is especially rough and knobbly.

PORT JACKSON SHARK

Like other members of the bullhead shark family, a Port Jackson shark is perfectly suited to a life hunting on the seabed. Its patterned skin helps it stay hidden and the dark bands on its body even **mimic** shadows cast by sunlight passing through the sea.

Night Hunters

Port Jackson sharks hunt at night. They lie in wait for animals, such as starfish or octopuses, to pass by, or they swim close to the seabed, searching for prey. These sharks mostly use their sense of smell to find food.

Home Range

These sharks live along the coasts of Australia (except northern coasts) and nearby islands. Although they are not fished, they are often trapped in nets that have been put out to catch other fish.

This shark is unusual because its big, round nostrils are connected to its mouth.

On the Move

Bullhead sharks such as the Port Jackson don't just swim, they also use their fins to crawl along a rocky seabed. In the summer, they migrate closer to the shore where they lay their eggs.

The shark's pectoral fins are large and strong.

FRILLED SHARKS AND COW SHARKS

Frilled sharks and cow sharks are among the most ancient of all sharks. They closely resemble sharks that lived nearly 400 million years ago. There are only two types of frilled sharks and four types of cow sharks.

BITE-SIZE FACT

Scientists have found **fossils** of frilled sharks that lived in the oceans 95 million years ago.

Frilled shark

Strange Creatures

These sharks lead mysterious lives. Scientists do not know much about frilled sharks and cow sharks because they often lurk in the deep, dark, parts of the oceans. Those that live in cool oceans live closer to the shore than those that live in tropical waters.

Six Gills and Seven Gills

Most sharks have five pairs of gill slits, but cow sharks have six or seven pairs of gill slits and frilled sharks have six pairs. No one knows why these sharks have extra gills. A cow shark also has one very long tail fin and a large mouth.

Bluntnose sixgill sharks have up to 108 pups at a time. They are found in waters to a depth of 6,000 feet.

Cow sharks, like frilled sharks, have just one dorsal fin. They have broad heads and small eyes.

BROADNOSE SEVENGILL SHARK

Broadnose sevengill sharks live in cool, shallow water near land and hunt for fish, seals, and small whales to eat. The largest, oldest sharks move offshore and live in cooler, deeper water than young sharks. These sharks are also known as bluntnose sevengill sharks.

These sharks often have white and black speckles on their skin.

They often swim in cloudy water, where their prey cannot see them approach.

Teeth and Fins

These sharks have up to six rows of teeth, set in large jaws. The teeth on the upper jaw have jagged edges and the teeth on the lower jaw are comb-shaped. Unlike most sharks, these sharks and their close relatives have just one dorsal fin, not two.

64

Large and Fast

This is a powerful predator that may grow to more than 10 feet long. It is most active at night, attacking its prey with sudden speed. Broadnose sevengill sharks can live for up to 50 years. They are found in warm and cool seas, except the Mediterranean Sea and the North Atlantic Ocean. They are rare in the Indian Ocean.

They are fast swimmers, with long, powerful tails.

BITE-SIZE FACT

Bluntnose sevengill sharks often hunt large prey in packs. They can survive for several days without eating.

Breeding

Females are pregnant for about 12 months and they swim inshore to nursery areas when it is time to give birth. They can have more than 80 pups at a time, each one measuring 16-20 inches long.

FRILLED SHARK

Frilled sharks are so rare, there are only two species that have been discovered so far. They are three-six feet long and have needle-sharp teeth, a broad mouth, and a short snout. They are sometimes called eel sharks because of their long, slender body shape and long tail fin.

Lifestyle

Like most other sharks, frilled sharks live alone. However, they travel inshore to mate in spring. Female frilled sharks give birth to around ten pups at a time, and each one is about 16 inches long. Scientists think that these unusual sharks live for 50 years or more.

Dagger-Like Teeth

Frilled sharks usually swim with their large mouths open, exposing rows of large teeth. Each tooth has three long, dagger-like points, called cusps. Frilled sharks are predators of deep sea squid and bony fish.

Frilled sharks have 25 rows of razor sharp teeth.

Frilled sharks are named for their 12 frilly gill slits—six on each side of the head.

Habitat

Frilled sharks are mostly found near Japan, New Zealand, and in the eastern Atlantic Ocean. They prefer deep water, from 330 to 4,265 feet, and are benthic fish. This means they live on or near the seabed.

Frilled sharks live in the Eastern Atlantic ocean.

DOGFISH SHARKS

Dogfish sharks have two dorsal fins, which sometimes have sharp spines on them. They live throughout the world's oceans, and are the only sharks that are known to live in the cool waters near the poles.

A Portuguese shark.

Dorsal fin of a dogish shark.

Swimming Deep

Many dogfish sharks live near land, but others live in the deepest parts of the ocean. Portuguese sharks have been found at depths of nearly 3,000 feet, where few other animals can survive.

Varied Group

There are about 130 types of dogfish sharks. This large group includes little lantern sharks—that are able to glow in the deep, dark sea—as well as large, slow-moving sleeper sharks, that can grow to 26 feet.

Lantern shark. ├ – – – – – – – –

At Risk

Dogfish sharks were once very common, but they have been overfished, mostly for food, in more than 50 countries. They are slow-moving, which makes them easy to catch. They also have few pups at a time, which means that populations of dogfish sharks are slow to recover once they have fallen.

BITE-SIZE FACT

Lantern sharks are probably the smallest sharks in the world—they are often less than one foot long.

COOKIECUTTER SHARK

Most hungry sharks eat all of their prey, but cookiecutter sharks just take bite-sized chunks! They are named after the cookie-shaped holes they leave in their prey's flesh, and live in very deep water.

A cookiecutter's body is long and thin, with two small dorsal fins.

Cookiecutter mouth showing teeth.

Fatal Attraction

Cookiecutter sharks make their skin glow, which attracts fish to them. The shark then attacks the fish and holds on tight with its sucking lips and sharp teeth.

Big Bite

As its victim struggles to escape, the predator clamps its jaws tighter on its flesh and twists its body. Its teeth slice out a round chunk of food and the shark can then swim away to swallow its meal in safety.

BITESIZE FACT

Cookiecutters swallow their old teeth—so they can recycle the calcium in each tooth!

Speeding and Feeding

Cookiecutters have good eyesight, and can turn on the speed to chase their prey. The teeth in their upper jaw work like the prongs on a fork to hold their food in place while they bite!

GREENLAND SHARK

Greenland sharks live in the freezing waters of the Arctic. Like many other animals that live in cold places, these giant sharks move slowly and live long lives—to the age of 100 or more.

Hunting and Scavenging

Greenland sharks hunt almost anything, from small squid to whales and seals. They have about 100 little teeth, which they use to seize their prey. They also scavenge and they have been found with the carcasses of large land animals, such as reindeer, in their guts.

Almost Blind

Many Greenland sharks have copepods—small sea animals—attached to the front of their eyeballs. The copepods eat the transparent skin there and can make the sharks blind. This may be one reason why Greenland sharks sometimes scavenge instead of hunt.

Greenland shark with copepod parasite on its eye.

Toxic Shark

Greenland sharks can survive in icy Arctic waters because a chemical in their flesh works like an anti-freeze. This chemical also turns their flesh toxic, so it is **poisonous** to humans if it is eaten.

Although these sharks usually swim slowly, they can move with great bursts of speed when they hunt.

SPINY DOGFISH SHARK

The spiny dogfish shark is one of the most common sharks in the world. It is also known as the piked dogfish, the spur dogfish, and the blue dog. Scientists know more about this species of shark than almost any other.

A spiny dogfish has two sharp spikes.

Sharp Spikes

When a spiny dogfish is scared, it arches its back and attacks, using its venomous spines to wound an attacker. It has two of these spines—one in front of each dorsal fin.

Schools

Male spiny dogfish rarely grow beyond 39 inches long. Females are slightly bigger. They gather in large groups called schools, but each school has either males or females—but not both.

A school of sharks.

The skin is gray to brown and there is usually a line of white spots along the fish's side.

Habitat

Spiny dogfish sharks live worldwide, except in the warmest waters around the equator, and the cool polar seas. They are found near land, rather than the open ocean. Their nursery areas are near bays and **estuaries**, especially where the seafloor is soft mud.

CARPET SHARKS

Carpet sharks are usually found on the ocean floor, and are often colorful or patterned—just like a carpet! This clever disguise helps them to stay camouflaged.

A tasseled wobbegong.

Barbels of a carpet shark.

Special Senses

There are about 42 types of carpet shark. They have a pair of sensitive feelers, called barbels, around their mouths which help them sense objects on the seabed.

Types of Carpet Shark

This large and varied group contains seven families of shark: collared carpet sharks, blind sharks, longtailed carpet sharks, wobbegongs, nurse sharks, the zebra shark, and the whale shark.

Most carpet sharks hunt animals that live on, or near the seafloor.

BITE-SIZE FACT

Some carpet sharks can use their pectoral fins like limbs to "walk" along the seabed.

Sit and Wait

Most carpet sharks are slow swimmers. They either sit and wait for their prey, or creep up on them. However, they turn up the speed when they need to lunge forward and catch prey.

EPAULETTE SHARK

Epaulette sharks live in warm, shallow seas around the coast of Australia and islands nearby. An epaulette is a decoration on the shoulder of a jacket, and these sharks have decorative dark spots above their pectoral fins. There are different types of epaulette sharks, but they lead similar lives.

This type of epaulette shark is also known as the Indonesian speckled carpet shark.

Shy Creatures

This small, shy shark is a slow swimmer. During the day it hides among coral reefs. At night it hunts for animals on the seabed.

This speckled carpet shark is a type of epaulette. It often lurks beneath coral.

Quiet Lives

Epaulette sharks live near the seabed in shallow water, especially around coral reefs. They are slow swimmers and spend the day resting. They hunt at night, searching for animals on the seabed.

Spotty Bodies

Epaulettes have speckles, spots, or blotches of color on their bodies. Their pups often look quite different, with bands of color as well as spots. These sharks have two dorsal fins, set far back, near the tail. They are less than 3.5 feet long when fully-grown.

Epaulette sharks, like this one from Papua New Guinea, have slender bodies and long tails.

79

NURSE SHARK

Most nurse sharks are about six feet long but these carpet sharks can grow to nine feet or more, including a long tail.

A school of nurse sharks.

Close Knit

They often gather in groups of up to 40 sharks. They lie very close to each other, sometimes even piling on top of one another!

The nurse shark is common in the warm waters of the Atlantic Ocean and eastern Pacific Ocean.

Eating Habits

Nurse sharks use their large mouths to suck up food from the seabed, and they are even able to suck a sea snail out of its shell. Their favorite prey includes bony fish and stingrays, as well as invertebrates, such as squid. They particularly rely on their sense of smell to find food—if they cannot smell, they cannot hunt.

Nurse sharks have rounded dorsal fins and very long tail fins.

Shark Enemies

Nurse sharks may be large but they are slow swimmers and not aggressive. Other sharks—such as lemon sharks, bull sharks, and tiger sharks—successfully hunt them.

SPOTTED WOBBEGONG

Wobbegongs are some of the most colorful and patterned of all sharks. Their strange appearance helps them to stay hidden on the seafloor. The name "wobbegong" probably comes from the language of the Aboriginal Australians, those **indigenous** to Australia.

BITE-SIZE FACT

These sharks can clamber out of the water to reach tide pools.

A spotted wobbegong is almost invisible as it swims near the seabed.

Bigger Than Most

Spotted wobbegongs can grow up to 10 feet long, and are larger than most other types of wobbegong.

Big Bite

Wobbegongs have very powerful jaws and sharp, fang-like teeth—perfect for a mixed diet of crabs, lobsters, bony fish, and octopuses. These fish can push their jaws forward to suck food into their mouths.

Whiskery barbels hang from this shark's mouth. They help it hide among seaweed.

Family Life

Wobbegongs have about 20 pups at a time, after a long pregnancy of up to two years. These sharks can probably live to 30 years or more.

ZEBRA SHARK

Zebra shark pups have stripes or spots, which are a type of **camouflage**. Camouflage helps them hide among seaweed and in shallow water. As they grow, they swim out to the deep ocean, and some of their stripy markings fade away.

Most zebra sharks grow to about 6.5 feet long.

Spots and Stripes

When zebra sharks are young, they have stripes. When they get older, they have spots.

Young sharks are called pups. This pup still has its stripes.

Finding Food

Zebra sharks wriggle inside rocky holes to find small fish and crabs to eat. They often lie on the seabed with their mouths open and facing the current. Zebra sharks have small, spiked teeth.

Habitat

Zebra sharks live in the Indian and south Pacific Oceans, in warm water and close to shore—although pups often stay in deeper water. Zebra sharks are often found around coral reefs and they lay their eggs on the seabed, then attach the eggs with tufts of hair.

The holes above this shark's small mouth are nostrils.

GROUND SHARKS

This is the largest group of sharks, with at least 291 types of ground shark discovered so far. Most of these sharks are the typical shark shape, with a torpedo-shaped body that is **streamlined** for fast movement through water.

BITE-SIZE FACT

Nearly all sharks live in the oceans and seas, but some ground sharks are able to live in rivers, too.

Types of Ground Shark

This group includes the large and important **requiem** shark family, such as tiger sharks, blue sharks, silky sharks, and blacktip and whitetip sharks. It also includes hammerheads, smooth dogfish, leopard sharks, swellsharks, catsharks, and false catsharks.

Special Features

Ground sharks have a special lower eyelid that can cover the eyeball to protect it. They also have two dorsal fins on their slender bodies. Most ground sharks are two-three feet long, but some species grow much bigger than this.

The lower eyelid protects the eye when a shark attacks its prey.

Ground sharks can live in both deep and shallow water.

Most ground sharks are small to medium sized, with round, slender bodies.

Eggs and Pups

Many ground sharks, such as catsharks, lay eggs. The eggs stay on the seafloor where they grow for up to a year before they hatch. Others give birth to their pups.

BLACKTIP REEF SHARK

Coral reefs provide a good habitat for many ground sharks, including blacktip reef sharks. The reefs are home to plenty of small animals for the sharks to hunt, including invertebrates and shoals of fish.

These reef sharks often gather in groups near the shore.

Energetic Hunters

Blacktip reef sharks live in warm, shallow waters. They are very good hunters and sometimes use a special technique in which they leap out of the water and rotate up to four times before splashing back in. They eat fish, squid, and crustaceans.

BITE-SIZE FACT

This shark can
swim in water
that is just 12
inches deep!

Peaceful Creatures

Blacktip reef sharks are often seen near
the coast, but they usually swim away
quickly if they are disturbed. They live in
the warm waters of the southern Pacific
Ocean, the Indian Ocean, and the eastern
Mediterranean Sea.

Toursim

Divers enjoy watching blacktip
reef sharks swimming around coral
reefs, but these precious habitats
are being damaged by climate change
and pollution. As a result, the number
of all reef sharks is expected to fall.

A diver gets
close to a
reef shark.

BLUE SHARK

These are the most graceful of all sharks. Blue sharks live in the open ocean, and they are one of the world's most widespread sharks. They can survive in all the world's oceans, including the warmest edges of the Arctic and Southern Oceans.

Blue sharks swim near the surface, looking for fish to eat.

This predator feeds on shoals of fish, such as anchovies.

Long Distances

Blue sharks go on long journeys, called migrations. They can travel thousands of miles across the ocean because their bodies are a streamlined shape. The longest recorded migration for any blue shark is a journey of 3,740 miles from the coasts of New York to Brazil.

BITE-SIZE FACT

Many blue sharks are killed each year due to overfishing.

Filter Feeders

Although blue sharks are predators of fish and squid, they are also able to filter feed, like the whale shark, because their gills can trap small animals such as shrimp. Blue sharks also scavenge on big animals such as whales.

Life Cycle

Female blue sharks of the Atlantic Ocean mate in the western Atlantic before swimming across the seas towards European waters, following the ocean currents. They give birth in the eastern Atlantic and have 30-50 pups at a time.

BULL SHARK

This broad, strong shark is known for its aggressive nature. Bull sharks are described as "short tempered," which means they are always ready for a fight!

Warm Waters

Bull sharks are mostly found in tropical areas, where the water is warm. However, they also live around the southern coasts of Africa and Australia, and as far north as Canada.

Sensitive Senses

Bull sharks have poor eyesight. Instead, they rely on a superb sense of smell. Like other sharks, they have a sensitive line that runs along their body, called the lateral line. This detects movement and vibrations in the water.

Lateral line

BITE-SIZE FACT

Some experts believe that the bull shark is the deadliest shark in the world.

Freshwater Fancy

Almost all sharks live in seas and oceans, where the water is salty. Bull sharks are more adaptable. They live in shallow coastal waters, but they also swim up rivers, and have even been found in **freshwater** lakes. Spotting a bull shark can be difficult, because they often swim in cloudy water.

Bull sharks usually live and hunt on their own.

GREAT HAMMERHEAD SHARK

Of all the ground sharks, hammerheads are the most bizarre. Their massive, broad heads make these powerful predators easy to identify. Great hammerheads live in warm waters, especially around coral reefs.

Great Eyesight

A hammerhead's head is huge and wide, with eyes positioned right at the very ends. This shape probably helps the predator move through water and change direction. The position of its eyes helps the shark focus on its prey more easily, and figure out how far away it is.

Fight for Life

Hammerheads can live for about 30 years, but few of them reach that great age. They are endangered, which means that they are at risk of becoming **extinct** because too many have been fished from the sea. They are also **cannibals**, and adults often prey on young hammerheads.

A hammerhead's nostrils are far apart, helping it to sense the direction of different smells.

Hammerheads sway their heads from side to side as they swim —detecting hidden fish or stingrays to eat.

More Hammerheads

There are at least eight more species of hammerhead sharks: wingheads, malletheads, scoopheads, bonnetheads, smalleye hammerheads, smooth hammerheads, and two species of scalloped hammerhead. One species of scalloped hammerhead was only discovered in 2013.

Scalloped hammerheads have distintive heads that look like a scallop shell

BITE-SIZE FACT

Hammerheads like to feast on venomous stingrays, and even eat the venom-filled tails!

GRAY REEF SHARK

Sometimes divers and snorkelers come face-to-face with some of the world's most threatening sharks—gray reef sharks. They are medium-sized sharks that live in the warm waters of the Indian and Pacific Oceans.

Gray reef sharks are strong swimmers.

The body is gray, but the edge of the tail fin is black.

Social Sharks

Most sharks are **solitary** animals and live alone. Gray reef sharks, however, often swim in groups in quiet spots during the day, with as many as 20 other sharks. At night, they go their separate ways to hunt.

Fishy Feasts

Gray reef sharks feed on squid, octopus, and small, shelled animals such as shrimp and lobsters. Colorful coral fish also make a good meal for reef sharks but, like other prey, they often stay in the stony coral for safety.

Gray reef sharks have a keen sense of smell.

Stay Away!

When a gray reef shark is feeling threatened, it raises its snout, arches its back, and swims in a swaying motion. This menacing behavior warns enemies to move away—or prepare to be attacked.

LEMON SHARK

Lemon sharks are large coastal sharks of the Pacific and Atlantic Oceans. They prefer to live in warm, shallow waters near land, especially during the day. At night they swim to deeper water and they can also rest on the seabed.

A lemon shark has a wide, flat head.

Staying Safe

Pups are born between April and September. Each female can give birth to up to 17 pups at a time. They stay in their nursery areas for several years where they are safe from adult lemon sharks, which sometimes eat them.

Lemon sharks get their name from the yellow-brown color of their skin.

Sharksuckers

Remoras, or sharksuckers, are long, thin fish with a sucker on the top of their head. They use this to stick to a shark or other large fish and hitch a ride. Remoras feed off any scraps that the shark does not eat and also help sharks to stay healthy by eating their parasites. Some lemon sharks have been known to eat remoras.

A remora fish attached to a lemon shark

BITE-SIZE FACT

Lemon sharks sometimes swim up rivers. They can adapt to different levels of salt concentration.

Magnetic Sensors

Lemon sharks have small eyes and poor eyesight. The coastal waters where they live are often cloudy, so eyesight is not a great help in finding prey. Instead, these fish have special magnetic **sensors** in their snout, which help them find fish and shelled animals on the seabed.

OCEANIC WHITETIP SHARK

Oceanic whitetip sharks swim in the deep open ocean, far from land. They were once common in the warm waters of the world, but their numbers have fallen in recent years.

Striped pilot fish often swim near sharks. They eat scraps of food dropped by the sharks.

The pectoral fins are extremely long and wing-like.

Agile Swimmers

These predators swim slowly as they cruise, looking for prey. They speed up when they are chasing fish. This shark uses its pectoral fins to lift up its body as it moves through water.

The fins on the oceanic whitetip shark have rounded, white tips.

Lifecycle

Females usually give birth to a litter of up to five pups at a time, each one measuring about two feet long. As they age, females have bigger litters. The adults grow up to 10 feet long.

BITE-SIZE FACT

These sharks often swim in groups, following fishing boats.

Hunting Skills

When oceanic whitetips hunt, they become very aggressive and fight off any other sharks that come to feed. They have large, triangular teeth for grabbing and biting prey.

Oceanic whitetips have an acute sense of smell.

PyJAMA SHARK

Pyjama sharks have long, dark stripes. They are also known as striped catsharks. They live around southern Africa, and can swim in water up to depths of around 330 feet.

BITE-SIZE FACT

Pyjama sharks often eat shark eggs and they hunt other small sharks, too.

Nocturnal Hunters

During the day, pyjama sharks hide in caves and between rocks. They hunt at night, making them **nocturnal** creatures, and their favorite foods include shelled animals, worms, and small fish.

Small Pups

These small sharks have pups that are just six inches long when they hatch from their eggs. A female lays just two eggs at a time—in sticky egg cases—and they attach themselves to seaweed while the pup grows inside.

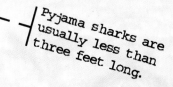

Pyjama sharks are usually less than three feet long.

Eating Squid

The long, dark stripes on a pyjama shark's back help it to hide on the seabed. They sometimes lurk, unseen, in places where squid lay their eggs. Once the squid have finished laying eggs, the sharks can begin to feast.

When a pyjama shark is scared, it rolls its body into a ball.

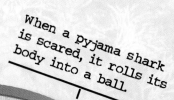

SILKY SHARK

Silky sharks are large sharks with long, pointed snouts and big eyes. They usually live in the open oceans and they prefer warm water, especially where they can find plenty of food. They often chase schools of tuna.

BITE-SIZE FACT

Mothers give birth to their pups in coral reefs, where there is lots of food for them.

Teeth

Silky sharks have small jaws and their teeth are triangular in shape. When a silky shark is scared, it arches its back and bares its teeth. This shark is curious and often approaches boats and divers. It has been known to attack people when it is scared.

The pectoral fins are long and slender.

Speedy Swimmers

These large predators live in warm, open oceans, anywhere that they can find lots of fish to eat. They are fast swimmers, and often swim alongside large groups of scalloped hammerhead sharks.

Scales

The scales on a shark's skin are made of tooth-like scales, called denticles, which are very tough, and rough to the touch. Silky sharks have small, closely-packed denticles, which make their skin feel smooth spend silky.

SWELLSHARK

Swellsharks are also known as puffer sharks, or balloon sharks. They have a surprising way of staying safe under the sea!

Swellsharks lie on the seabed, waiting for prey to pass by.

BITE-SIZE FACT

Swellsharks lay eggs, which attach themselves to seaweed or a reef.

Unusual Defense

When a swellshark is scared, it gulps water which makes its body swell up to twice its normal size. This scares any predators away.

Home Waters

Swell sharks only live in the eastern Pacific Ocean, from California to Mexico and Chile. Their favorite habitat is the rocky seabed with plenty of algae where eggs and pups are safe from predators.

Most types of swellshark are less than three feet long.

A swellshark's egg is called a mermaid's purse.

Catshark

Swellsharks are catsharks. There are about 160 species of catsharks (which are a type of ground shark), making them the largest group of sharks in the world. Catsharks can be recognized by their catlike eyes.

TIGER SHARK

Meet the terrifying tiger shark—one of the most dangerous sharks in the world. These predators have been compared to garbage cans because they will try to eat almost anything!

As well as having a powerful bite, tiger sharks have a very sharp sense of smell

Hungry Hunters

Tiger sharks are hungry, fearless hunters that come close to the shore in search of food. They spend most of the day slowly cruising through the water, but can suddenly burst into speed when they spy something tasty. They hunt sea turtles, **clams**, stingrays, sea snakes, seals, birds, and squid.

Scavengers

These sharks are scavengers, which means they are not fussy eaters and will feast on dead meat. They have been found with bottles, lumps of wood, potatoes, car tires—and even drums—in their stomach!

Tiger sharks are sometimes called "Bins with fins."

They are called tiger sharks because their skin is marked with dark stripes and spots.

BITE-SIZE FACT

Tiger shark teeth are serrated, like a saw. As the sharks bite, they pull their head from side to side and saw the flesh.

On the Move

Tiger sharks swim out to the open ocean in the day and come closer to shore at night. They are strong swimmers and often travel long distances.

MACKEREL SHARKS

This is the most famous of all shark groups, as it includes fast and deadly hunters such as the great white shark. There are 15 species of mackerel shark, but not all of them are deadly predators—two species are filter feeders.

Many mackerel sharks have long, round bodies with pointed snouts.

Different Sizes

Mackerel sharks range in size from the little crocodile shark—about three feet long—to giant basking sharks, which can be more than ten times as long!

Warm Blood

Many mackerel sharks are able to keep their bodies warm, even in chilly seas. This means they are able to survive in cold places where other sharks cannot hunt.

Mackerel sharks have two dorsal fins, a large mouth, and a fast, powerful body.

Mixed Group

Mackerel sharks are found worldwide, from warm to cool waters, and they eat a range of food from tiny plankton to whales and dolphins.

BASKING SHARK

The enormous mouth of a basking shark is large enough to hold a child. Fortunately, a basking shark has no interest in human prey because it only eats tiny plankton!

BITE-SIZE FACT

Basking sharks often swim near the surface of the sea, and can even leap out of the water!

The largest basking sharks weigh up to 21 tons—five times as much as an elephant!

Breathing Underwater

The huge slits on the side of a basking shark's head are called gill slits. Fish use gills instead of lungs to breathe underwater. Water, which contains oxygen, passes into their mouth and out through the gills. Basking sharks also use their gills to feed. Sieve-like plates in the gills trap any plankton in the water.

Mystery Shark

Sharks are mysterious creatures, and scientists need to find out much more about their lifestyles. It is known that basking sharks go on long journeys in spring and summer, but no one knows for sure where they disappear to from November to March.

Basking sharks are slow-swimming and unaggressive.

Water and plankton gush into the shark's huge gaping mouth.

Cold Waters

Basking sharks do not mind cold water and they even migrate to the icy Arctic Ocean where they can find large amounts of plankton to eat. They swim at the water's surface with their huge mouth open.

GOBLIN SHARK

Goblin sharks are mysterious fish that hunt in the deep oceans. They are slow swimmers that search for small fish in the dark. Scientists know very little about these sharks because very few have ever been found.

The jaw can move forwards to grab fish.

Different Teeth

The shark's teeth at the front of its jaws are very long and dagger-like. That is the perfect shape for grabbing small, slender fish. The teeth at the back of its jaws are the right shape for grinding up bones or shellfish.

Lifecycle

No one knows where these sharks breed, or how many pups they have at a time. Scientists think they may grow bigger than 10 feet, and they may live long lives as they probably have no predators.

The body is soft, flabby, and pink-white.

The strange snout is long and flat.

Hunting

The strange snout may be part of the shark's electro-sense. It may be used to detect the movement of any other animals nearby—that is a useful skill for an animal that lives in the pitch dark.

GREAT WHITE SHARK

Great whites have a reputation as vicious killers, but they are smart sharks with strong, stout bodies, super senses, and big appetites. They are certainly well equipped to hunt, catch, and kill their prey.

Powerful and Deadly

Great whites are special sharks. They are big and powerful, they swim at high speeds and over great distances, and they are extremely skilled hunters. They can detect a single drop of blood in nearby water.

Great whites have 50-60 large teeth in each row. When one tooth falls out, it is quickly replaced.

Bite and Shake

When a great white takes a bite of its prey, it shakes its head from side to side. As it does so, the large triangular teeth saw through prey, chomping off large pieces of meat.

A great white's bite is three times more powerful than a lion's bite.

Great whites hunt fish, seals, and seabirds. They hunt seals at dawn, when seals cannot see them coming.

Great whites usually swim alone, but are sometimes seen hunting in pairs or small groups.

Huge Beasts

Great whites are some of the largest sharks in the ocean. Pups are already five feet when they are born, and they can grow to more than 16 feet long.

117

MEGAMOUTH SHARK

This shark was first discovered in 1976. Since then, only about 65 have been seen. It lives in deep water, where it is dark and very cold. Megamouths are filter feeders and they mostly eat plankton and small fish.

The megamouth shark's mouth is so large, it could swallow small children.

Big Appetite

The megamouth shark is so called because of its huge mouth and rubbery lips. It swims slowly with its mouth wide open. This lets the shark take in massive amounts of water to trap prey, such as shrimp, in its gills.

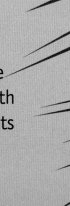

Slow Swimmer

Unlike other sharks, which have muscular bodies, the megamouth shark has a flabby body. It does not need to swim quickly to catch fish, which is why its muscles are weaker than most other sharks.

The megamouth shark has a very large head.

Growing Up

No one has yet seen a newborn megamouth pup, and no one knows where their nurseries are. Adult megamouths grow to about 16 feet long—about the length of a car.

PORBEAGLE SHARK

Most porbeagles live in the North Atlantic Ocean where they can grow to more than 10 feet long. A population of smaller porbeagles lives in the southern Pacific Ocean.

Porbeagles have good eyesight and may even see some colors.

BITE-SIZE FACT

Porbeagles normally give birth to just four pups at a time.

Warm Muscles

Fish—including most sharks—have cold bodies, but porbeagles keep their muscles warm. This means they can live in cold seas and swim fast to chase their prey.

Curious Sharks

Porbeagles are intelligent sharks that are often curious about boats and divers, and swim up close to investigate. However, they are not dangerous to humans.

Each tooth has a large, bladelike part, and a "mini tooth" on each side of it.

Ocean Swimmers

Porbeagles spend the summer close to shore and near the surface of the water. In the winter, they swim out to the open oceans and may go to depths of 2,300 feet.

Porbeagles are fast, powerful swimmers.

121

SAND TIGER SHARK

Sand tiger sharks have long, spiky teeth so they are also called spotted ragged-tooth sharks. They live in shallow water, even swimming close to shore in depths of just three feet.

Sand tiger sharks are slow, strong swimmers.

BITE-SIZE FACT

Sandtiger pups often eat their brothers and sisters while they are still inside their mother's body.

Protected

Although sand tigers are not usually fished for food, their numbers have fallen and they are now protected in many areas. This means fishing boats should not trap or catch them.

Gulping Air

Sand tiger sharks are the only sharks that are known to come to the surface of the water to gulp air. The air stays in their stomach where it helps them float in shallow water.

A sandtiger's teeth are the perfect size and shape for gripping slippery fish.

This hungry sandtiger shark is hunting for small fish to eat.

Pack Hunters

Sand tigers grow to more than 10 feet long. They hunt in groups of up to 80 sharks at a time. These sharks often swim close to sandy shores and are shallow water predators.

SHORTFIN MAKO

The shortfin mako is the fastest of all sharks, speeding through the ocean at around 42 miles per hour. Their slender, long bodies, and small, bullet-shaped heads are streamlined—which means they are perfect for slicing through water.

These powerful fish are packed with muscles. They can move in bursts of very high speed to pursue their prey.

Big Leaps

Shortfin makos are not only fast swimmers, they can also jump out of the water—leaping more than 20 feet into the air to avoid predators.

Speedy Scales

The scales on a shark's skin are shaped to make a good surface for water to flow over it smoothly, helping a shark swim fast. Makos have super-speedy scales, strong tails and powerful swimming muscles. They also have sharp, long teeth to help them hold onto their prey.

Rows of long, thin teeth are ideal for grabbing hold of slippery fish and squid.

BITE-SIZE FACT

"Mako" means "shark" in Maori—the native language of New Zealand.

Lifecycle

Female shortfin makos do not give birth to their first litter of pups until they are about 17 years old. They are pregnant for up to 18 months, and litters contain up to 25 pups.

Makos are often chased and killed for sport.

THRESHER SHARK

There are three species of thresher shark: the pelagic thresher, the bigeye thresher, and the common thresher shark. They live in the warm, tropical waters of the open ocean as well as coastal areas.

Thresher sharks have long pectoral fins.

Good Swimmers

These sharks are strong swimmers and they can travel through the oceans at top speeds without tiring. They often leap out of the water.

Stun and Eat

Threshers have bizarre tails, which are extremely long. A shark's tail fins are called the caudal fins. They are made up of two parts, called lobes. The upper lobe of a thresher's caudal fins can be as long as the rest of the shark's body.

Half of this shark's length is its tail!

A thresher shark swims near the seabed.

Stunning Sharks

Threshers use their long, whip-like caudal fins to attack prey. They sometimes work together to herd shoals of fish before whacking them with their tails. The tails stun—or even kill—the prey.

WHALE SHARK

The whale shark is the largest fish in the ocean. Some grow as long as a bus and weigh a massive 16.5 tons. Adult whale sharks may grow to about 39 feet long.

The whale shark's mouth is 4.5 feet wide!

Huge Mouth

The whale shark feeds by swimming along with its mouth wide open. It takes in huge mouthfuls of water, which it sieves through its gills. All the fish, squid, krill, and plankton in the water are eaten.

The whale shark has a beautiful pattern on its body.

Live Young

Female whale sharks do not lay eggs. Instead, they give birth to as many as 300 baby sharks at one time. Whale shark nurseries have been found in the Red Sea and the Indian Ocean, but many whale sharks probably swim to remote islands and give birth there, where they are undisturbed by human activity.

Whale shark pup

Whale Shark Mysteries

Scientists still know very little about this giant fish. They do not know how or where they mate, and no one has witnessed whale sharks give birth. Very few whale shark pups have ever been seen in the wild.

FOSSIL SHARKS

Humans have only been on the planet for about two million years, but sharks have been swimming in the oceans for 400 million years! Scientists study modern sharks and use fossils of ancient sharks to discover the story of how sharks have changed over time.

Ancient Creatures

Scientists know about ancient sharks by studying fossils. These are the remains of animals that lived long ago. They have been turned to stone over millions of years.

Fossil of small shark.

Bone Puzzles

Scientists who study fossils are called paleontologists (pay-lee-on-tol-oh-jists). They use clues from the shape and position of bones to try and figure out how ancient creatures looked and lived.

The Golden Age

Sharks ruled the oceans about 280-360 million years ago and there were many different types of sharks. That time is now called the "Golden Age of Sharks."

Dorsal spine of an ancient shark.

Shark tooth fossilized in stone.

MEGALODON

Megalodons were massive sharks that first appeared in the world's oceans about 15 million years ago. In many ways, they were similar to modern sharks, such as the great white.

Megalodon wasn't the only giant shark to patrol the ocean.

Huge Beast

This powerful beast may have grown to 50 feet long, more than three times the size of a great white shark! It probably hunted large animals, such as other big sharks or whales.

Mega-Fossils

Megalodon fossils have been found on every contintent, except Antarctica. Paleontologists have figured out how big the Megalodon shark was by looking at fossils of its backbones and its teeth. Using these clues, they have reconstructed a giant Megalodon jaw that is 11 feet across!

Megalodon teeth.

Mega-mystery

No one knows why megalodon died out, but it may have lost the battle for survival when the world's climate changed, becoming much cooler.

Megalodon was possibly the biggest fish to ever live.

SHARKS UNDER THREAT

Many sharks are killed for their fins, which are used to make shark fin soup. Large sharks breed slowly and, if they are overfished, their numbers quickly fall. The United States and the European Union have banned **shark finning** to protect the shark population. In some places, sharks are threatened because there is too much fishing in general, and not enough food left for the sharks to eat.

On organized trips, divers can swim with sharks.

Don't Be Scared of Sharks!

Many people are afraid of sharks, but these amazing animals are an important part of the ocean system. Shark tourism encourages people to get to know sharks better. On some coral reefs, food is left out to attract sharks so divers can get close to them. Shark tourism earns money for local people and that means that the sharks are less likely to be killed.

Shark Fin Soup

Only the fins are needed for shark fin soup. The rest of the shark's body is simply thrown back into the sea. Shark fin soup is a speciality dish in China.

A shark's dorsal fin.

A great white swims close to a boat.

DISCOVERING SHARKS

Scientists observe sharks by diving with them, often inside safety cages. They also track sharks' behavior and movements with tagging.

A scientist interacts with a lemon shark.

Tagging

An electronic device called a **tag** is attached to a shark's fin. The tag sends out signals which scientists use to follow the shark's journey, finding out how far it travels and where it goes.

BITE-SIZE FACT

A blue shark tagged near New York was found 16 months later, 3,600 miles away, off the coast of Brazil.

Find Out More

There are many organizations that support sharks and work hard to make sure they survive. They have websites with more information on shark species, and they provide up-to-date news on the work scientists are doing to protect them.

This diver is swimming with a whale shark.

A diver can watch and film a great white shark from the safety of a cage.

Marine Parks

Many countries want to protect the oceans and the animals that live there, so they have set aside special areas where fishing boats cannot go. Sharks can live in these marine parks in safety, and tourists can visit them.

GLOSSARY

adapt
how an animal changes to suit its environment

algae
simple, plantlike living things, such as seaweed

ampullae of Lorenzini
tiny sensors near the front of a shark's head. These detect electrical signals produced when an animal moves

aquarium
a glass tank filled with water in which living aquatic animals and plants are kept

baitfish ball
when a large group of fish swim together in a tightly packed spherical shape, usually when threatened

camouflage
an animal's coloring that blends in with its background

cannibal
animals that eat others from the same species

carcass
the body of a dead animal

cartilage
a strong, flexible fibre in animal's bones. Shark skeletons are made from cartilage

clam
a type of shellfish

crevice
a narrow gap in a rock or wall

current
the flow of water that moves
through the ocean

denticles
tooth-like scales on a
shark's skin

dorsal fin
a fin on the back of a fish,
whale, or dolphin. Most sharks
have two dorsal fins.

estuary
the mouth of a river

extinct
when the last remaining animal
of a species has died

filter feeders
sharks that use their gills to
gather small animals out of
the water

fossil
trace of a plant or animal
that lived long ago, preserved
in the Earth's crust, as rock
or ice

freshwater
water without salt in it, such
as that found in lakes and
rivers

gill slits
openings (slits or gaps) on
a shark's body where water
passes through

gills
organs inside the body of
a fish used for breathing
in water

global warming
a rise in the average
temperature of Earth's
atmosphere

gravel
loose, small pebbles and
stones

habitat
the place where an animal
lives

indigenous
a person who is native
to a particular place

invertebrate
an animal without a backbone

krill
tiny, shrimp-like creatures

lateral line system
a system of sense organs
found in sharks and other fish,
that detect movement and
vibration in water

magnify
make something look much
bigger than it really is

mangrove
a type of tree which grows
in shallow, coastal waters

microscopic
too tiny to see without an
instrument called a
microscrope

migration
a journey made each year to
find food or breed

mimic
to copy or imitate the
behavior of another animal

moray
a type of eel that is mainly
found in warm waters and
coral reefs

nocturnal
active at night

nostrils
The holes that lead into
a nose or snout

parasite
an animal that grows and
feeds on or in another animal
and causes it harm

pectoral fins
pair of fins on either side of a fish, whale, or dolphin

plankton
small animals and plants that float in the oceans, carried along by the ocean currents

poison
something that can harm or even kill

pollution
when something toxic is introduced into the environment and has a harmful effect

predator
an animal that hunts other animals to eat

prey
an animal that is hunted and eaten by other animals

pup
the young of a shark

requiem
a large family of sharks that give birth to live young

scavenge
to feed on dead or decaying matter or waste

school
a group of sharks

sensors
organs in an animal that respond to stimuli such as light or magnetism

shark finning
the act of removing some or all of a shark's fins for produce, such as shark fin soup or medicine

shoal
a group of fish

snout
the part on an animals face that sticks out, containing the nose and mouth

solitary
living alone, or away from other members of the same species

species
a group of individuals which have the same appearance and are able to breed and produce young together

spines
sharp spikes attached to a shark's fins

squid
a type of fast-moving sea creature with eight arms and two tentacles

streamlined
a smooth, slim shape that is able to move quickly through water

submersible
a vehicle used to explore underwater

tag
a small electronic device attached to an animal that sends out electronic signals. This means data on the animals' movements can be collected

INDEX